VOCAL SELECTIONS

FROZEN

MUSIC FROM THE MOTION PICTURE SOUNDTRACK

CONTENTS

ISBN 978-1-4803-9158-1

Disney characters and artwork © Disney Enterprises, Inc.

WONDERLAND MUSIC COMPANY, INC.

DISTRIBUTED BY

HAL•LEONARD®
CORPORATION

7777 W. BLUEMOUND RD. P.O. BOX 13819 MILWAUKEE, WI 53213

In Australia Contact:
Hal Leonard Australia Pty. Ltd.
4 Lentara Court, Cheltenham, Victoria, 3192 Australia
Email: ausadmin@halleonard.com.au

Visit Hal Leonard Online at **www.halleonard.com**

FROZEN HEART

Music and Lyrics by KRISTEN ANDERSON-LOPEZ
and ROBERT LOPEZ

Strike! for ___ love and strike for ___ fear. See the beau - ty sharp and sheer.

Split the ice ___ a - part, ___ and break the fro - zen

Faster

D5

heart. Watch your step! Let it go! Rr -

hyup! Ho! Watch your step! Let it go!

DO YOU WANT TO BUILD A SNOWMAN?

Music and Lyrics by KRISTEN ANDERSON-LOPEZ
and ROBERT LOPEZ

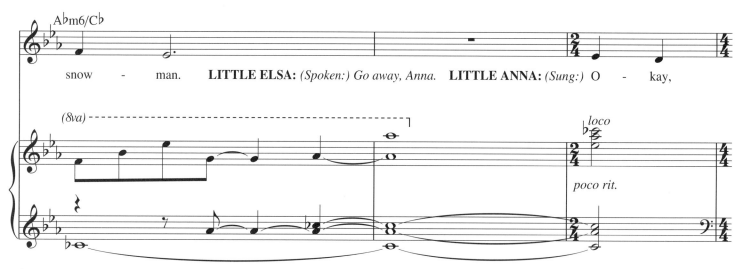

snow - man. **LITTLE ELSA:** *(Spoken:)* Go away, Anna. **LITTLE ANNA:** *(Sung:)* O - kay,

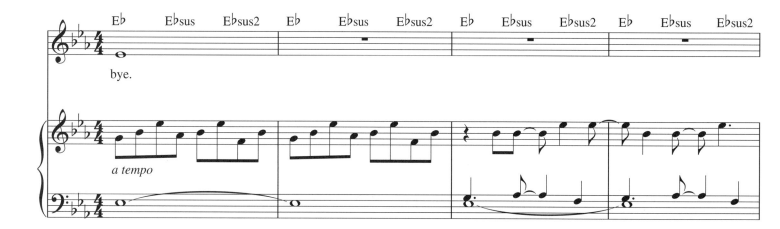

bye.

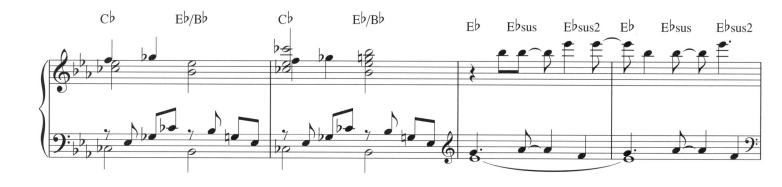

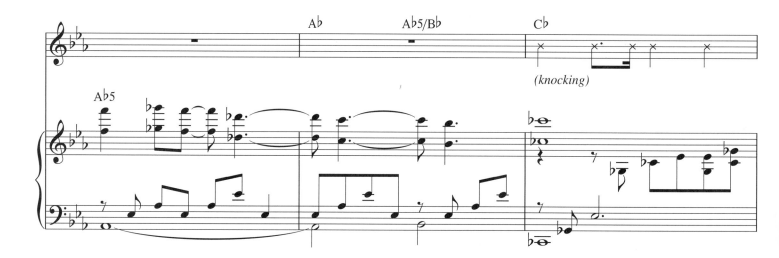

(knocking)

A little faster

YOUNG ANNA:
Do you want to build a snow-man? Or ride our bike a-round the halls? I think some com-pan-y is o-ver-due; I've start-ed talk-ing to the pic-tures on the walls. *(Spoken:)* Hang in there, Joan! *(Sung:)* It gets a lit-tle lone-ly, all these emp-ty __ rooms, _ just watch-ing the hours tick

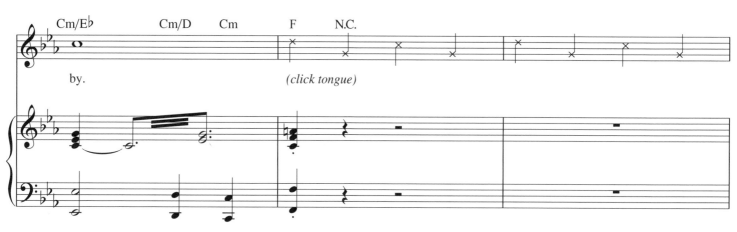

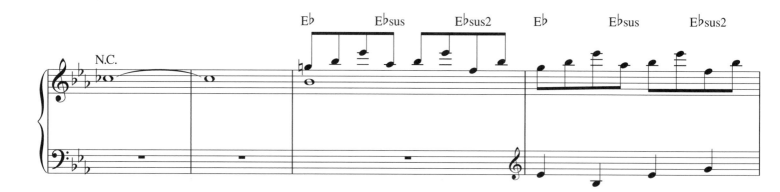

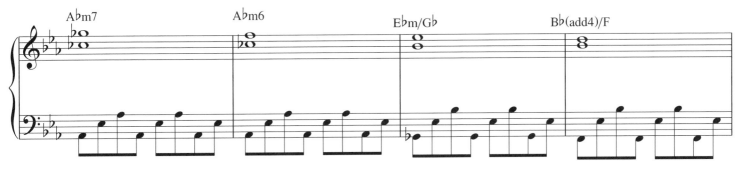

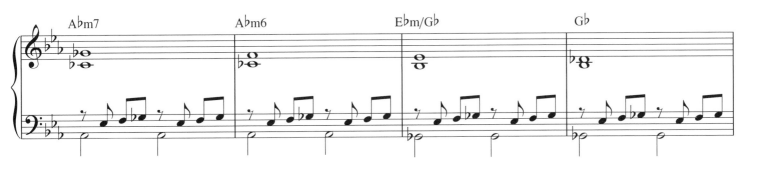

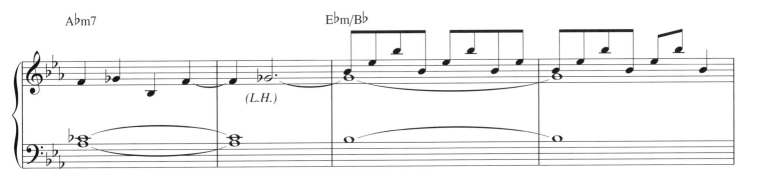

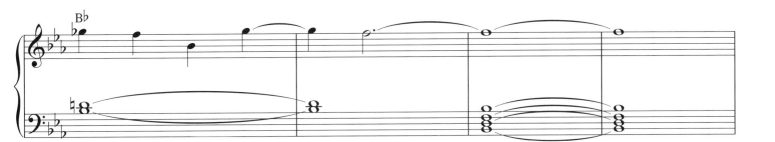

A little slower, tenderly

(knocking) **ANNA:** (Spoken:) Elsa? (Sung:) Please, I know you're in there.

Peo-ple are ask-ing where you've been. They say, "Have cour-age," and I'm

try-ing to; I'm right out here for you, just let me in.

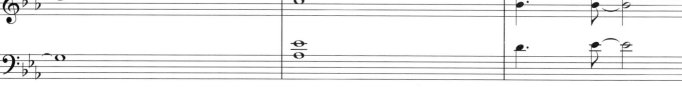

We on-ly have each oth-er; it's just you and me.

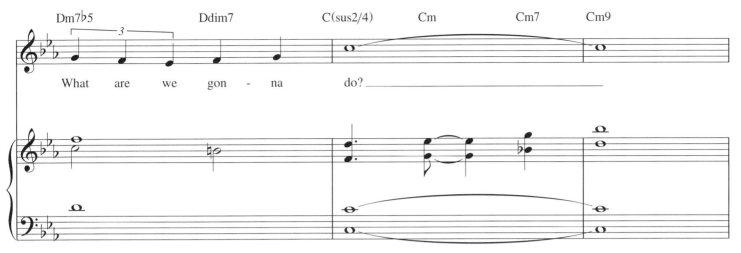

What are we gon - na do? _____

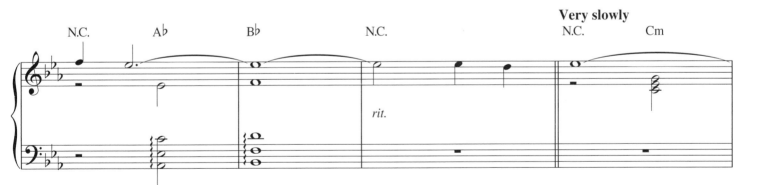

Slower

Do you want to build a snow - man?

Very slowly

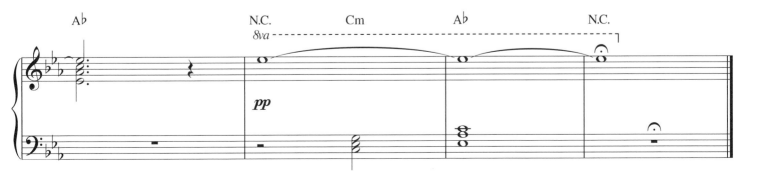

FOR THE FIRST TIME IN FOREVER

Music and Lyrics by KRISTEN ANDERSON-LOPEZ
and ROBERT LOPEZ

With excitement

ANNA: The win-dow is o - pen! So's _ that door! _ I
did-n't know they did that an - y - more. _ Who knew we owned _ eight thou - sand sal - ad
plates? For years I've roamed _ these emp - ty halls. _

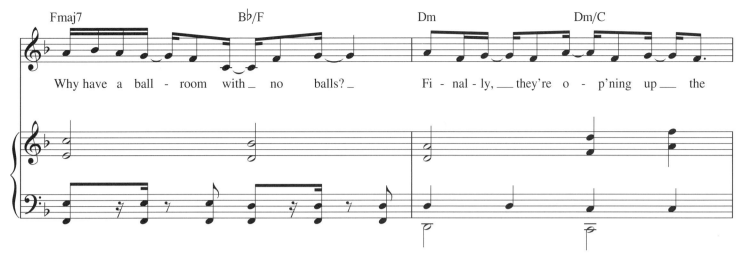

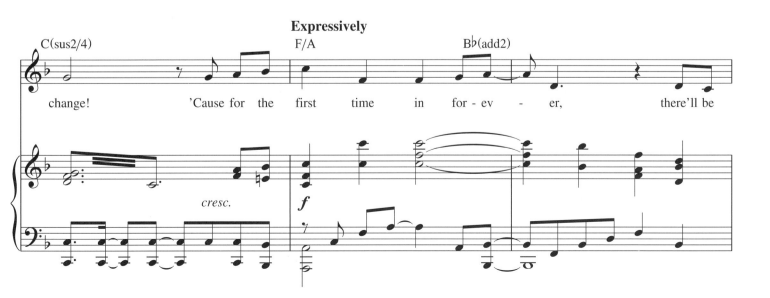

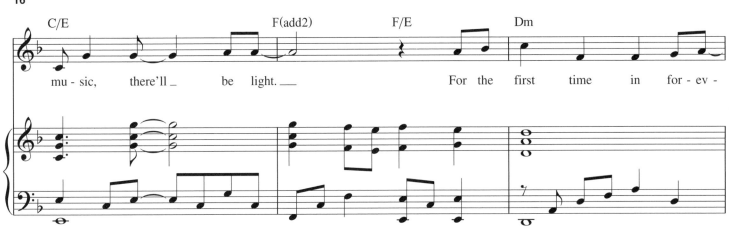

mu - sic, there'll _ be light. _ For the first time in for - ev -

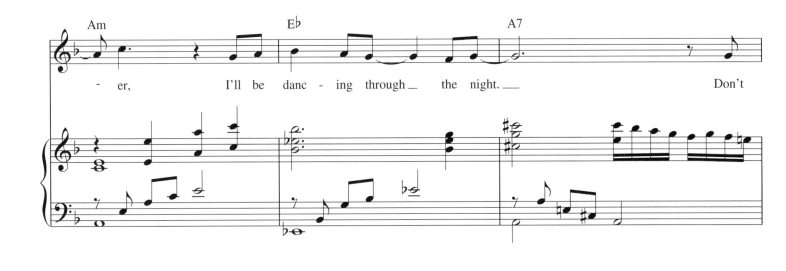

- er, I'll be danc - ing through _ the night. _ Don't

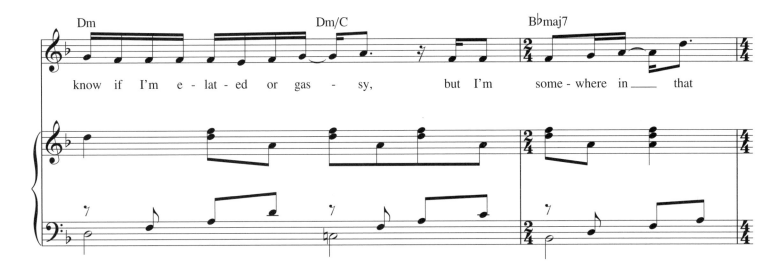

know if I'm e - lat - ed or gas - sy, but I'm some - where in ___ that

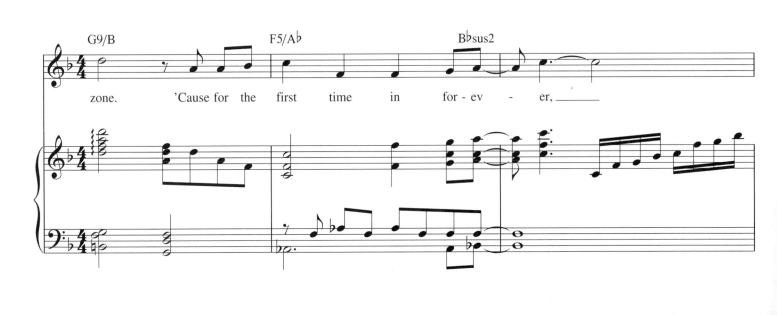

zone. 'Cause for the first time in for - ev - er, ___

Excited again

I won't be __ a - lone. __ *(Spoken:) I can't wait to meet everyone.* *(gasp) What if I meet...*

THE one? *(Sung:)* To - night, i - mag - ine me, gown __ and all, __

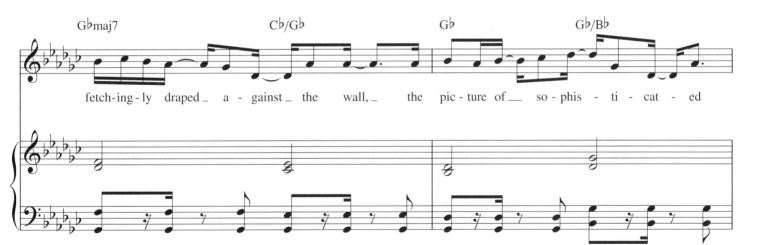

fetch - ing - ly draped __ a - gainst __ the wall, __ the pic - ture of __ so - phis - ti - cat - ed

grace. I sud - den - ly see __ him stand - ing there: __ a

beau - ti - ful strang - er, tall __ and fair. __ I wan - na stuff __ some choc - 'late in __ my

face! But then we laugh and talk __ all eve - ning, which is

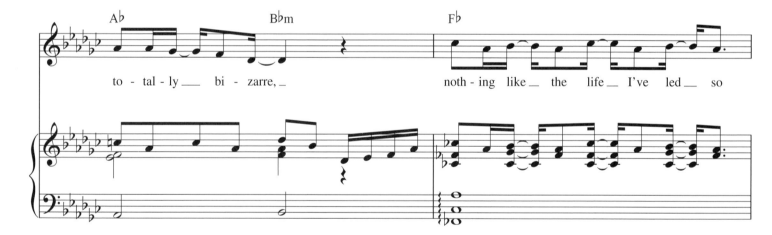

to - tal - ly __ bi - zarre, __ noth - ing like __ the life __ I've led __ so

far. For the first time in for - ev -

-er, there'll be mag - ic, there'll _ be fun. ___ For the

first time in for - ev - er, I could be no - ticed by __ some - one. _

And I know it is to - tal - ly cra - zy to

dream I'd find _ ro - mance, but for the first time in for - ev -

-er, _____ at least _ I've got _ a chance. _

Db7sus

Gb5 **Db/F**

8va - - - - - -

dim.

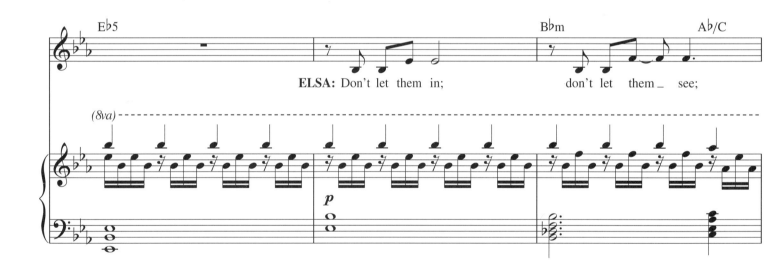

Eb5 **Bbm** **Ab/C**

ELSA: Don't let them in; don't let them _ see;

(8va) - - - - - - - -

p

Db **Absus** **Abm/Cb**

be the good girl _____ you al-ways have to be. _

(8va) - - - - - - - -

loco

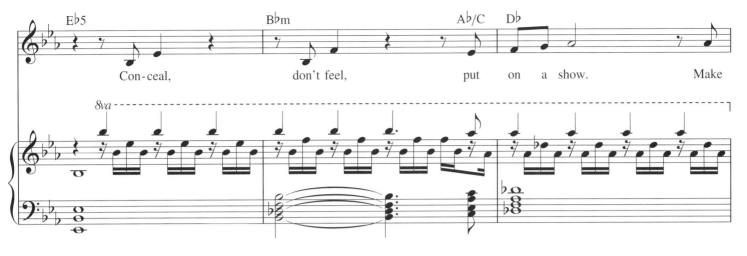

Con-ceal,   don't feel,   put on a show.   Make

one wrong move, and ev - 'ry - one will know.

But it's on - ly for to - day.   **ANNA:** It's on - ly for to - day!   It's ag - o - ny to

wait!   It's ag - o - ny to wait!   Tell the guards to o - pen up   the

A little broader

the gate! gate! For the first time in for-ev-

-er, I'm get-ting what I'm dream-ing of: __
ELSA: Don't let them in; __ don't let them see.

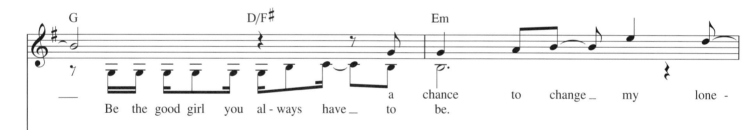

Be the good girl you al-ways have __ to be. a chance to change __ my lone-

-ly world, Con-ceal; a chance to find __ true love. __

I know it all ends to-mor-row, _____ so it

con-ceal, don't feel, don't let them know.

has to be _____ to-day. 'Cause for the first time in for-ev-

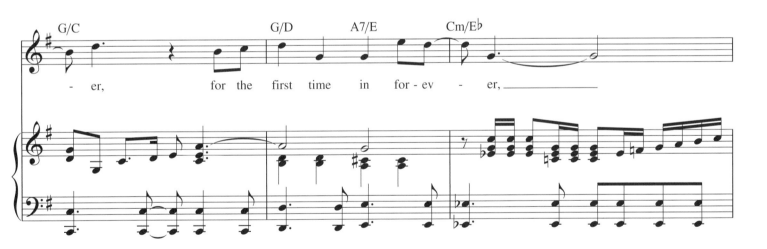

-er, for the first time in for-ev-er, _____

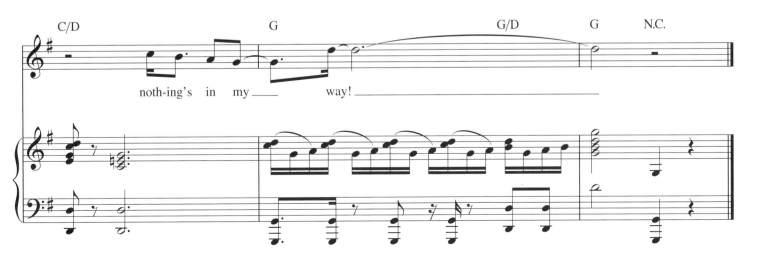

noth-ing's in my _____ way!

LOVE IS AN OPEN DOOR

Music and Lyrics by KRISTEN ANDERSON-LOPEZ
and ROBERT LOPEZ

Moderately, with a cheesy groove

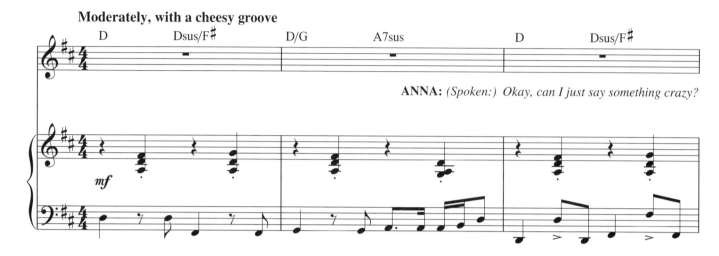

ANNA: *(Spoken:)* Okay, can I just say something crazy?

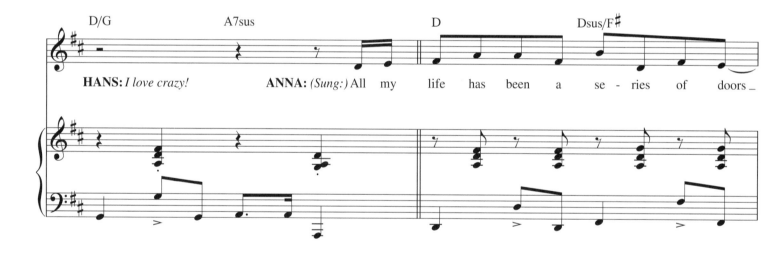

HANS: *I love crazy!*   ANNA: *(Sung:)* All my life has been a se-ries of doors

___ in my face, ___ and then sud-den-ly, I bump in-to you! _____

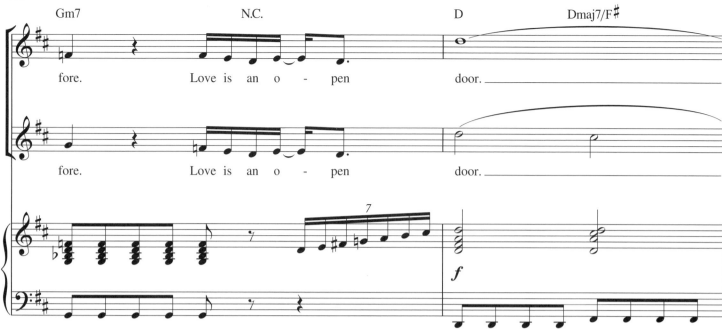

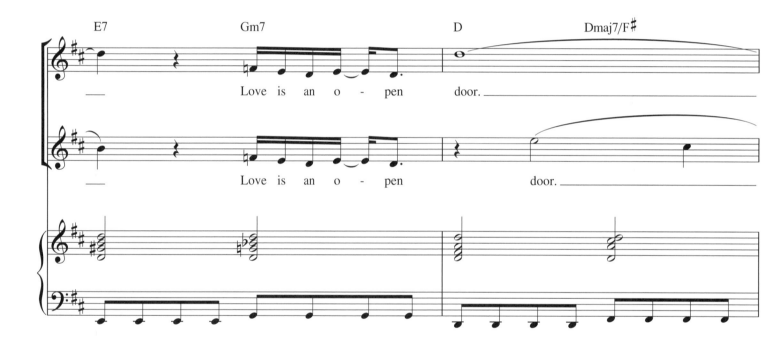

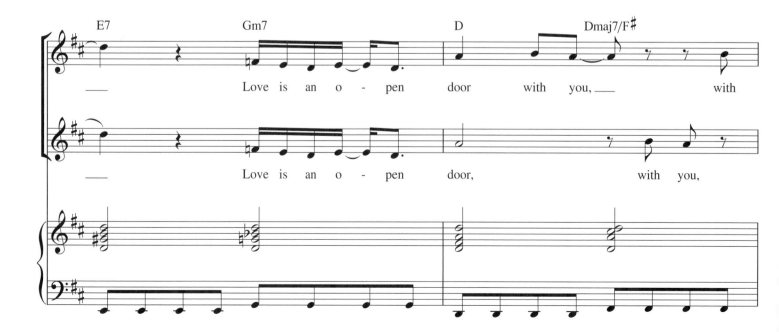

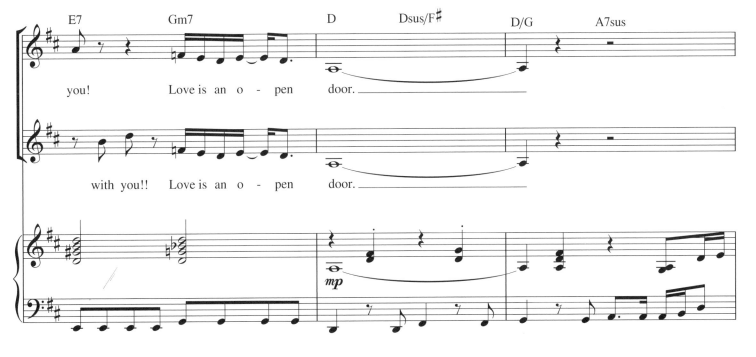

you! Love is an o - pen door. _____

with you!! Love is an o - pen door. _____

I mean, it's

What? ...sand - wich - es! I nev - er

cra - zy! We fin - ish each oth - er's... That's what I was gon - na say!

of the past; ___ we don't have to feel it an-y-more. ___

___ Love is an o - pen door. ___

___ Love is an o - pen door. _____ Life can be so __ much more with you! ___ With you!!! Love is an o - pen

more with you!! With you!!!! Love is an o - pen

door. ___

door. ___ (giggles)

(Spoken:) Can I say something crazy?

(Spoken:) Can I say something even crazier? Yes!

Will you marry me?

LET IT GO

Music and Lyrics by KRISTEN ANDERSON-LOPEZ
and ROBERT LOPEZ

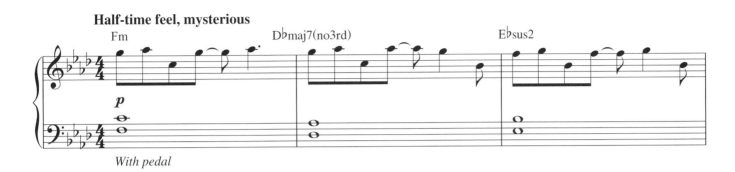

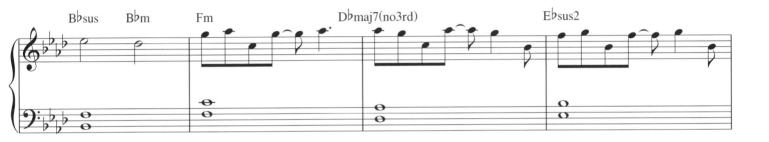

The snow glows white on the moun-tain to-night; not a

foot-print to be seen. A king-dom of i - so - la -

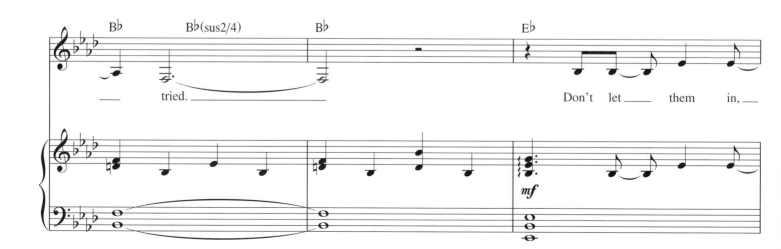

don't let them see; be the good girl you al-ways have to be.

Con-ceal, don't feel, don't let them know... Well, now they know.

Let it go,

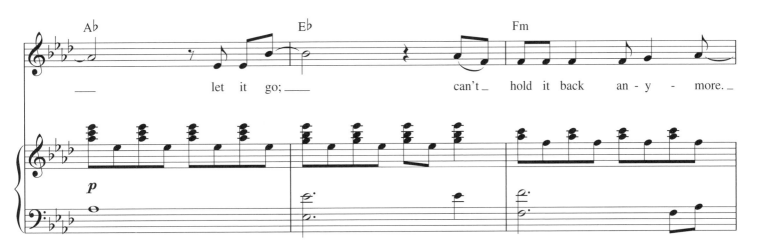

let it go; can't hold it back an-y-more.

Let it go, ___ let it go; ___ turn a - way ___

___ and slam ___ the ___ door. ___ I ___ don't ___ care ___

___ what they're going to ___ say; ___ let the

storm rage ___ on. ___ The cold nev - er both-ered me an -

Gaining confidence

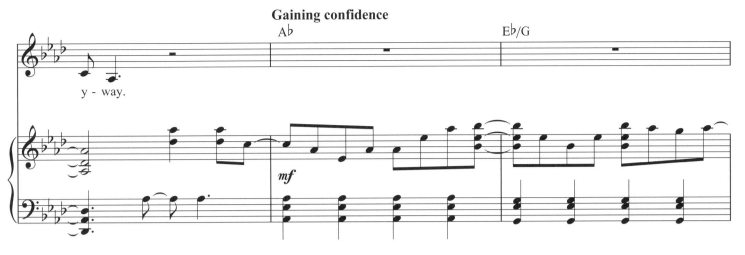

y - way.

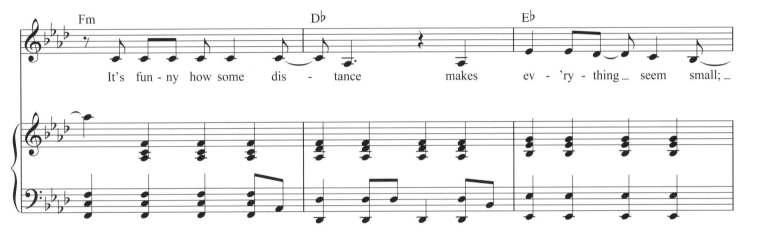

It's fun-ny how some dis - tance makes ev - 'ry-thing __ seem small; __

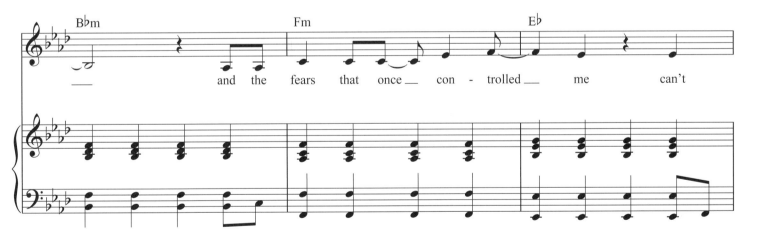

__ and the fears that once __ con - trolled __ me can't

get to me __ at all. __ It's time __ to see __

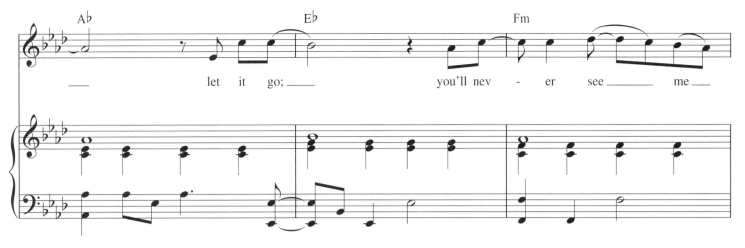

My pow - er flur - ries through the air _

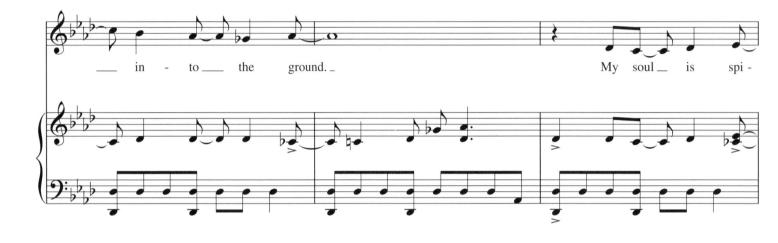

_ in - to _ the ground. _ My soul _ is spi -

- ral - ing _ in fro - zen frac - tals all _ a - round. _

And one _ thought cry - stal - li - zes like _ an i - cy blast: _

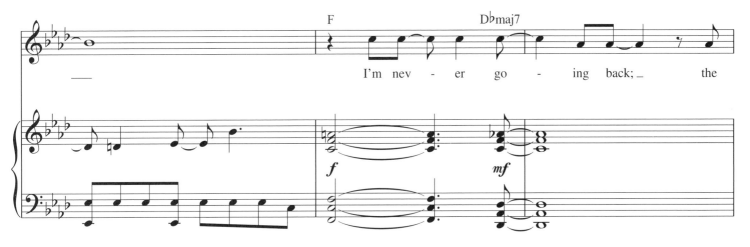

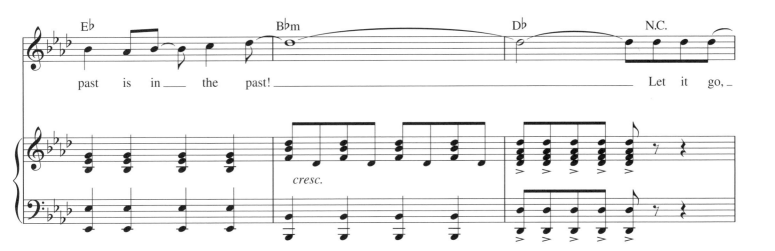

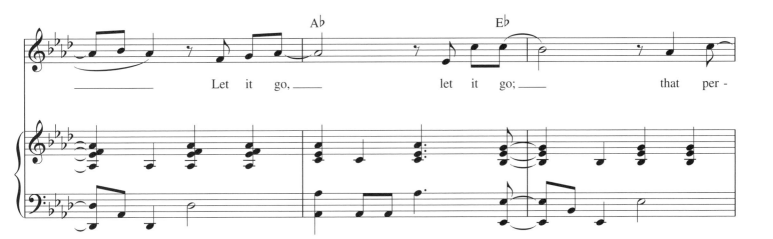

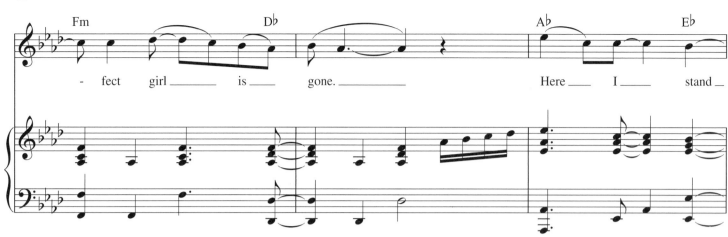

- fect girl _____ is _____ gone. _____ Here _____ I _____ stand _____

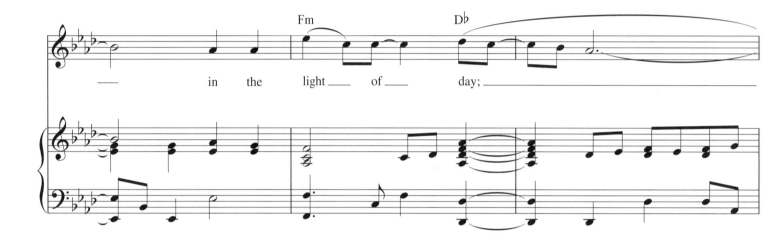

_____ in the light _____ of _____ day; _____

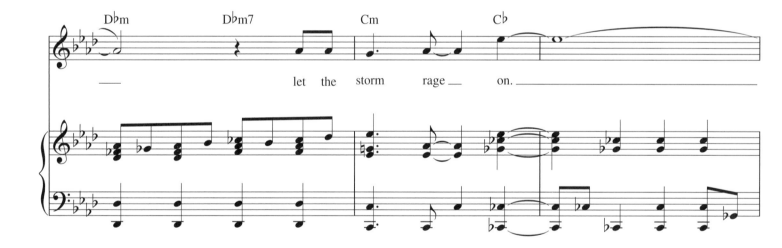

_____ let the storm rage _____ on. _____

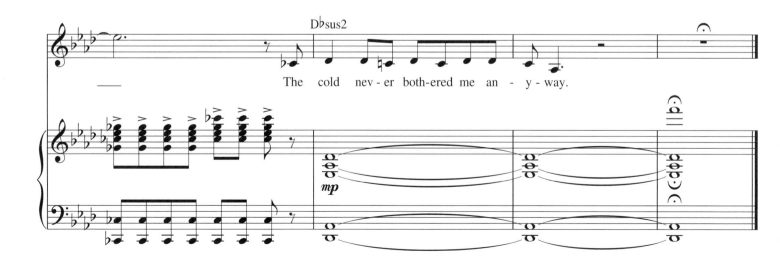

_____ The cold nev - er both-ered me an - y - way.

IN SUMMER

Music and Lyrics by KRISTEN ANDERSON-LOPEZ
and ROBERT LOPEZ

KRISTOFF: *(Spoken:)*
Really! I'm guessing you don't have much experience with heat.

Easy Swing, soft-shoe feel

OLAF: *(Spoken:) Nope! But sometimes I like to close my eyes, and imagine what it would be like*

With pedal

when summer does come. (sigh)   *(Sung:)* Bees - 'll buzz;

kids - 'll blow dan - de - li - on fuzz,   and   I'll be   do - ing what - ev - er snow does in

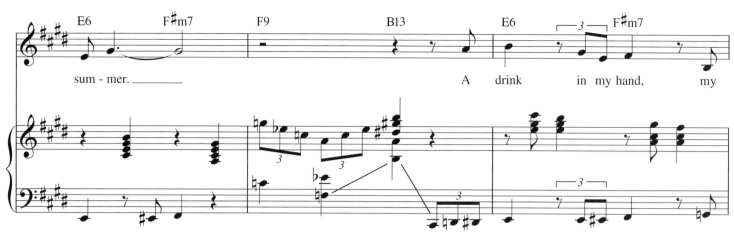

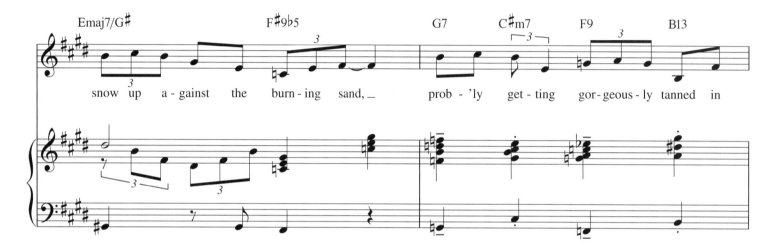

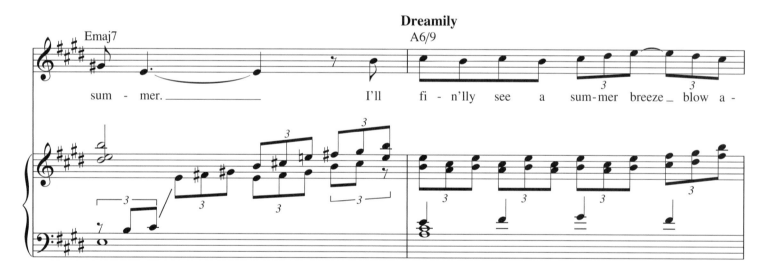

Dreamily

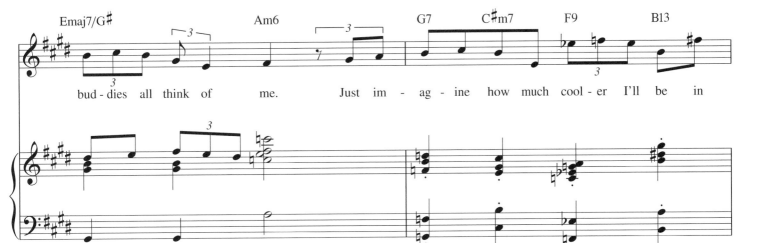

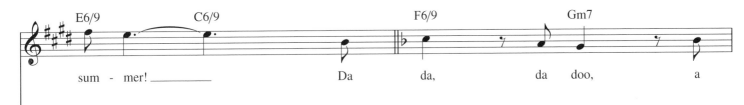

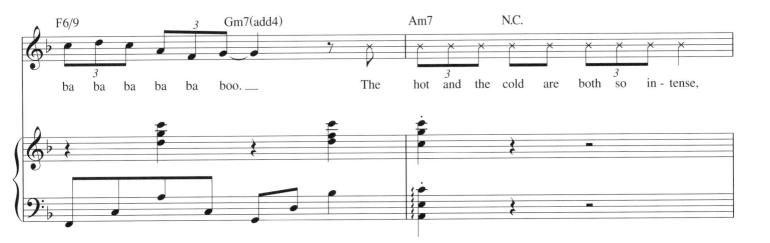

put 'em to-geth-er, it just makes sense. Rrrat dat dat dat dat dat

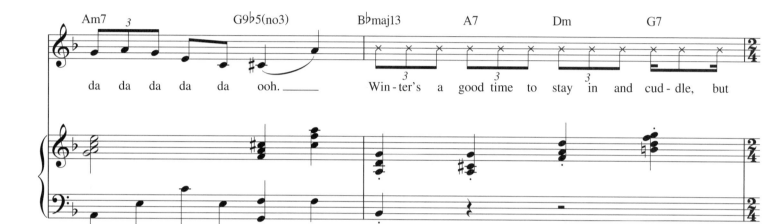

da da da da da ooh. ___ Win-ter's a good time to stay in and cud-dle, but

put me in sum-mer and I'll be a... *(Spoken:)* happy snowman!

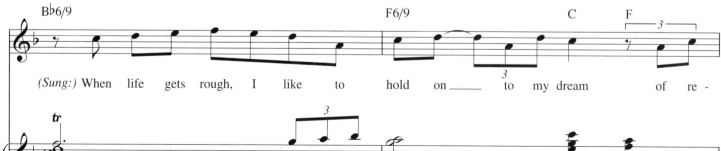

(Sung:) When life gets rough, I like to hold on ___ to my dream of re-

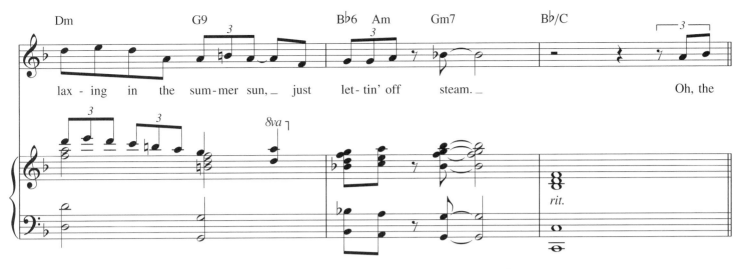

lax - ing in the sum-mer sun, _ just let-tin' off steam. _ Oh, the

Slower

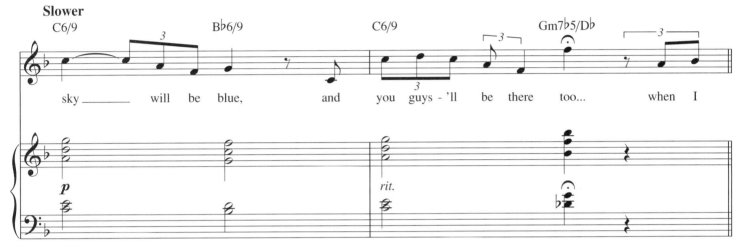

sky _____ will be blue, and you guys - 'll be there too... when I

Tempo I

fi - nal-ly do what fro-zen things do in sum-mer. _____

KRISTOFF: *(Spoken:)*
I'm gonna tell him.

Very broadly

ANNA: *(Spoken:)* **OLAF:** *(Sung:)* In sum-mer! _____
Don't you dare!

REINDEER(S) ARE BETTER THAN PEOPLE

Music and Lyrics by KRISTEN ANDERSON-LOPEZ
and ROBERT LOPEZ

FOR THE FIRST TIME IN FOREVER (REPRISE)

Music and Lyrics by KRISTEN ANDERSON-LOPEZ
and ROBERT LOPEZ

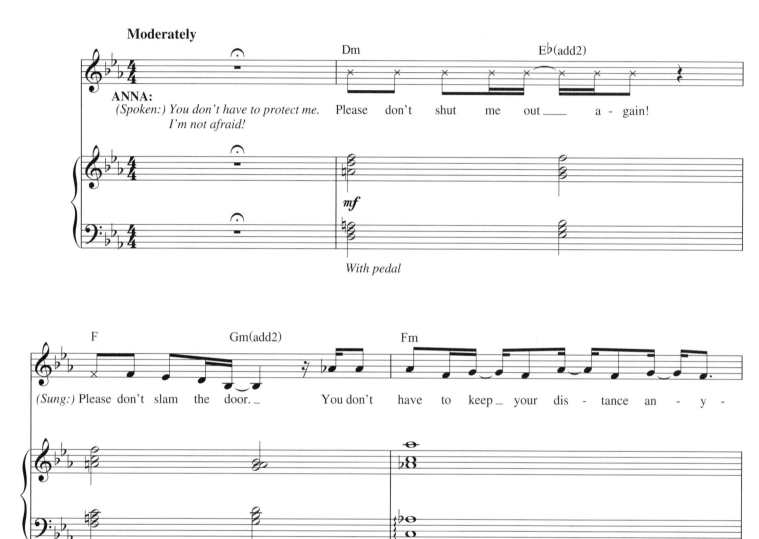

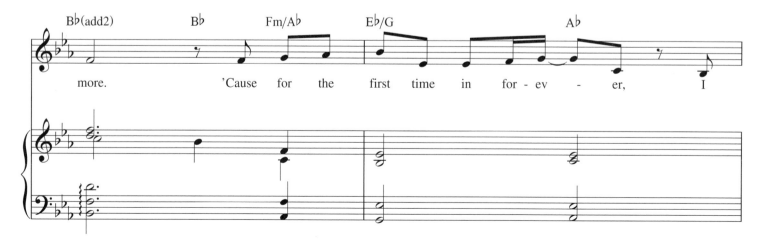

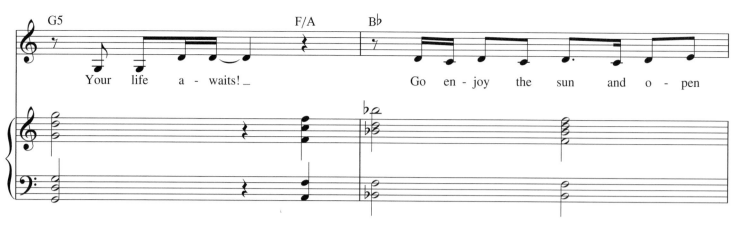

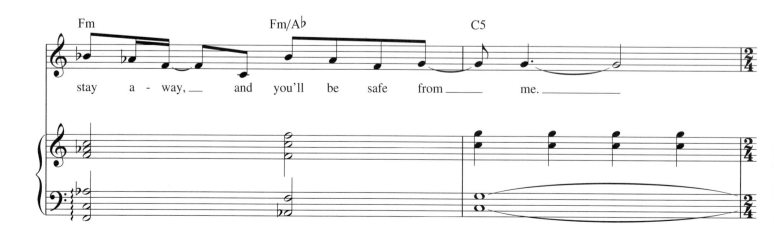

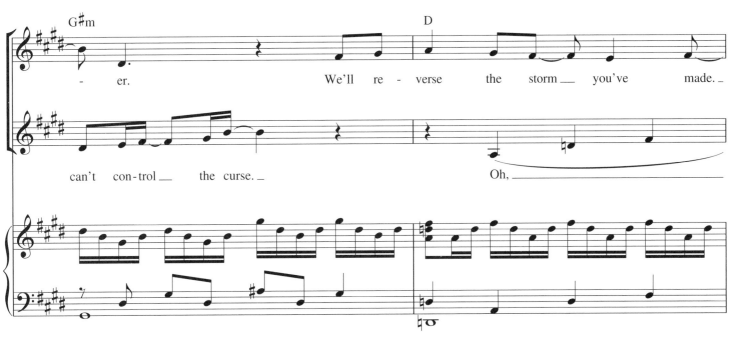

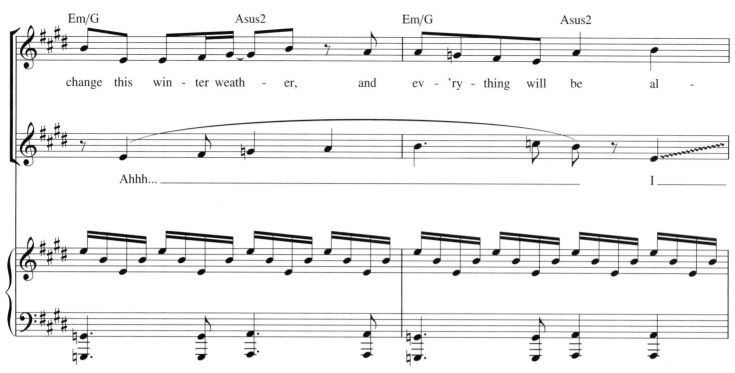

change this win - ter weath - er, and ev - 'ry - thing will be al -

Ahh... _____ I ____

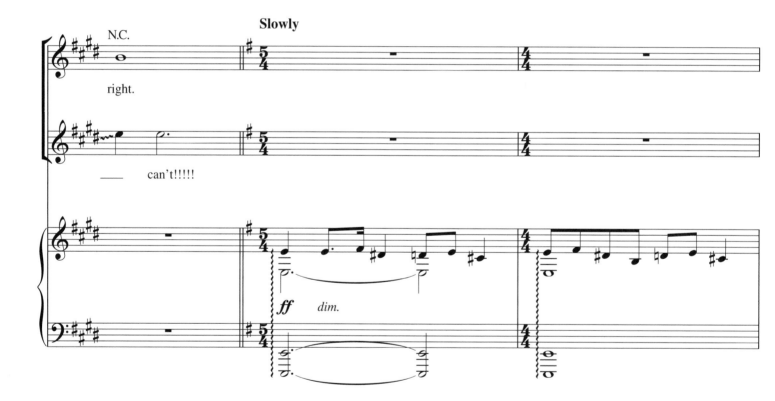

right.

____ can't!!!!!

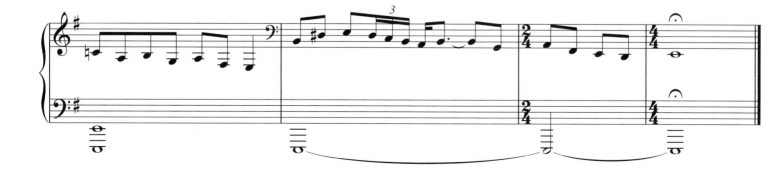

FIXER UPPER

Music and Lyrics by KRISTEN ANDERSON-LOPEZ
and ROBERT LOPEZ

With comic bounce

BULDA: *(Spoken:)* What's the issue, dear? Why are you holding back from such a man? *(Sung:)* Is it the

clump-y way __ he walks? **CLIFF:** Or the grump-y way __ he talks? Or the

FEMALE TROLL 1:

pear-shaped, square-shaped weird-ness of his feet? **MALE TROLL 1:** And though we

MALE TROLL 3: way that he ___ runs scared? Or that he's so-cial-ly ___ im-paired? **TROLL CHILD:** Or that he

on-ly likes ___ to tin-kle in ___ the woods? *(Spoken:) What?* **CLIFF:** *(Sung:)* Are you

hold-ing back ___ your fond - ness due to his un-man-ly blonde - ness? **FEMALE TROLLS:** Or the

way he cov-ers up that he's the hon - est ___ goods?

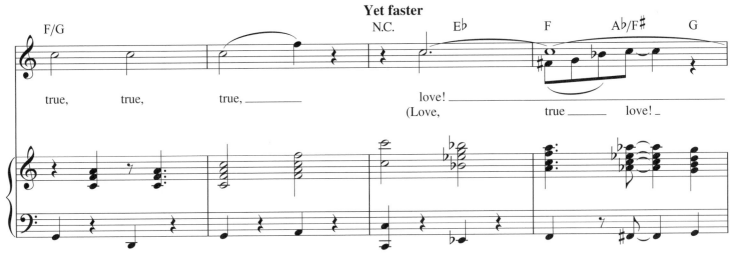

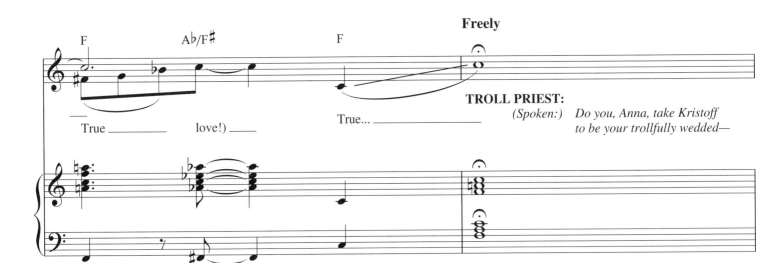